Eggshells to Objects

A New Approach to Egg Craft

Eggshells to Objects

A New Approach to Egg Craft

by Susan Riser Arnold

illustrated by the author

Holt, Rinehart and Winston / *New York*

10   9   8   7   6   5   4   3   2   1

        Library of Congress Cataloging in Publication Data
        Arnold, Susan.   Eggshells to objects.   Includes index.
Summary: Instructions for a variety of craft projects that can be
made with eggshells.
1.   Eggshell craft—Juvenile literature.   [1.   Eggshell craft.   2.   Handicraft]   I.   Title.
        TT896.7.A76   745.5   79-4328   ISBN 0-03-043981-7

To Denise and Rick,
masters of making something
out of nothing.

Contents

Introduction

An egg is a pure shape. It is perfectly formed, a smooth, round continuous line. Add a body to it, and presto, you have a puppet. Break off the end of an eggshell and you have an herb pot. Crack it into pieces, move the pieces around to form an image, and it becomes a mosaic. Fill egg shapes with plaster of paris, and an abstract wall hanging emerges. Apply plaster of paris to the inside walls of eggshell shapes, and the results are hard, durable objects.

For centuries people all over the world have been decorating eggs with symbolic motifs to support pagan and Christian beliefs. But, decoration is not the end. Instead of looking at an egg in terms of how to decorate it, try looking at it to see what it suggests to you.

For years I have been fascinated with the shape of an egg and its texture. The simplicity of the shape suggests so many possibilities for design. It can be subtracted from or added to, yet still retain the shape. It can be convex, concave, a container, a head, a sun. The texture is porous and receptive to a variety of substances such as paint, ink, glue, shellac, plaster of paris, dye, arabic gum, varnish, and many more. An egg is a natural material to decorate or to form into a visual expression, much like paper, wood, and rocks.

Try it and see for yourself. You will value the satisfaction of making something useful or decorative out of a simple egg. A little time and a few materials will produce inexpensive, beautiful hand made items that are gratifying to give, to receive, to display in a house, and most of all to make.

A design section at the back of the book gives patterns for tracing and design ideas.

The projects in this book should serve only as a guide. Let the perfect shape of the egg inspire in you ideas of your own to create useful objects and decorative egg crafts.

WHAT YOU NEED

Materials

The materials used in these egg crafts are as common as the eggs themselves. A further joy of egg craft is that the projects don't cost very much to make. The eggs used for the crafts in this book are extra large chicken eggs because they are the most common. But, if you have access to goose or ostrich eggs, by all means use these larger eggs for such projects as the herb pots, organizer tray, candlestick holders, modern furniture, tea set, sailboat, or even the simple painted egg. Following are most of the materials you will need in addition to the eggs:

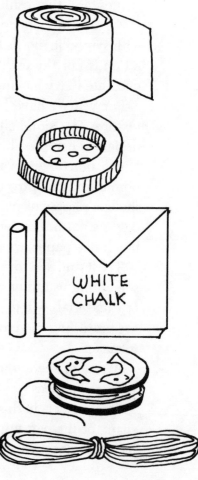

1. Brown paper tape, commonly used to wrap mail packages.

2. Buttons—plastic or wood with an indented center.

3. White chalk.

4. Clear fishing line, any size. These are sold in sporting goods stores, drug, and hardware stores.

5. Dyed straw—sold at arts and crafts stores. It is used to make hair on puppets. Yarn may be used in place of dyed straw.

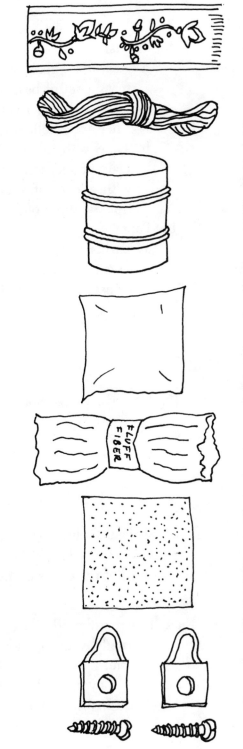

6. Embroidered ribbon—sold in fabric stores, arts and crafts, or specialty shops.

7. Embroidery thread—floss or thin crewel yarn.

8. Empty can—soup or coffee can or any other type of small can to mix plaster of paris and water together.

9. Felt, all colors (for puppet bodies).

10. Fluff fiber—sold at arts and crafts stores (for lion puppet).

11. Medium sandpaper—sold at hardware stores.

12. Metal picture hangers and screws—sold at drug and hardware stores sometimes as separate items.

13. Paints:
    a. Acrylics. These are sold in separate tubes or as a set of basic colors. Acrylics are diluted with water yet resist water when dry. They are excellent for egg crafts.
    b. Tube watercolors. They can be used in place of acrylics. If you use these, finish off with a coat of shellac to keep the color from washing off.

14. Paper.
    a. Carbon paper.
    b. Tracing paper or any thin paper that can be used to trace designs from book.
15. Paper towels.

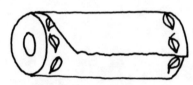

16. Plaster of paris. Sold at drug, craft, art, and hardware stores.

17. Shellac. Only a small quantity is needed. A 2-ounce bottle will be more than enough to do all of the crafts in the book.

18. Thin cardboard. Cardboard found in shirts returned by the laundry or something comparable.
19. Wiggle eyes. Sold at arts and crafts stores. (You can also make eyes from felt.)

14

20. Wire. A medium steel wire is easy to bend yet strong enough to retain its shape when a hollow egg is hung from it.

21. Yarn. Wool or acrylic.

Tools

Brushes

a. Flat nylon brush, 1 inch wide—this is made for acrylic paints. However, it works well with plaster of paris because it is more rigid than a common paintbrush.

b. Small round brush—a good sable brush in a size #2 is needed for painting small designs on eggs. It is much easier to use than a large brush or one that is in poor condition.

c. Paintbrush—any common watercolor or oil brush. These are used to paint large surface areas such as the stage set or an entire egg.

Elastic band—a wide elastic band, ¼ inch wide.

Glue

Knife—a kitchen knife that can be used to cut cardboard.

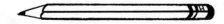

Pencil

Ruler—straight or cloth

Scissors

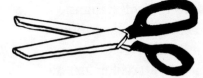

Spoon

Wire cutters

Safety pin

METHODS TO MAKE IT EASY

Hollowing Out an Egg

1. With a safety pin make a small hole in each end of a raw egg.
2. Place the egg over a bowl.
3. Hold egg gently though firmly and blow through one hole to force the entire egg through the other hole, into the bowl.
4. Slowly run water through the hollow egg to clean it out.

Using Plaster of Paris

Be sure to mix the plaster of paris in a clean, empty can. If the can has dried plaster in it, a new batch of plastic will set in the can in a few minutes. The consistency of the plaster for painting the inside of half-eggshells should resemble a thin pudding. In crafts which call for less water, the consistency should resemble a soft, grainy clay for molding. Most of the time the plaster sets in 20 minutes. It should be allowed to dry for a day after it sets. Since the plaster sets in 20 minutes, you will have to fill the required number of eggshells for a craft in that amount of time. If 20 minutes is not enough time, then cut the plaster recipe in half and fill in part of the items. Repeat the plaster recipe and fill in the remaining items. Each craft will have the appropriate plaster recipe for that individual craft.

Using Acrylic Paints

Acrylic paints usually come in tubes. Put a dab of each color you intend to use on a paper plate or a scrap of cardboard. Mix your colors some distance away from the clean pure colors. Rinse your brush before using a new color. Paper towels are handy for wiping off excess paint or water from the brush. A wet paper towel can also be used to wipe off any wet acrylic paint from the egg if you make a mistake.

Breaking an Eggshell

Almost all of the crafts require that part of the eggshell be removed. Breaking off the eggshell with a thumb and forefinger works just as well as any other method and is much easier than some. Break the shell gradually, taking small pieces off one at a time. The main concern is to keep the general line of the eggshell level or straight. The edge does not have to be smooth, because it will be sanded smooth later. You can only use one half of a single eggshell using this method.

Cutting an Eggshell

Cutting an eggshell with scissors has the advantage of yielding two half-shells from a single egg. Use curved manicure scissors to cut. Smear a thin layer of glue over the area you plan to cut. Let glue dry. Pierce the eggshell (with the tip of scissors) just above the line you are going to cut. Cut through the eggshell slowly and deliberately. Make little cuts instead of trying to make one long cut.

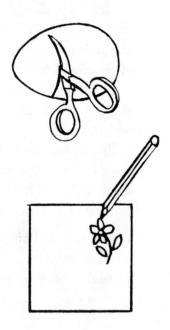

Tracing and Transferring a Design From Book

EGG

1. Place a sheet of thin paper that you can see through on the design or pattern you plan to

use from the back of the book. Hold the paper still and trace the lines with a pencil.

2. Take a piece of carbon paper that is slightly larger than the traced design and place it ink side down on the egg. Hold the egg in your left hand if you are right-handed. Hold the carbon paper in place with the index finger and thumb of your left hand.

3. Place the tracing over the carbon paper in the position you would like the design to appear on the egg. Hold it in place with the same fingers.

4. Trace over the lines with a pencil. There is no need to press hard to transfer design to egg.

5. Remove papers. The design will be on the egg in ink and ready to fill in with paint.

FABRIC

1. Trace the design from the book onto a thin piece of paper.

2. Turn the paper empty side up. Cover it with white chalk. Blow off chalk residue.

19

3. Place the paper with chalk side against fabric and design on top. Trace over the lines of the design with a pencil. Be careful not to move the paper while tracing.

4. Lift paper off fabric. The lines of the design will be on the fabric in chalk. Carefully brush off any chalk residue from fabric with your hand.

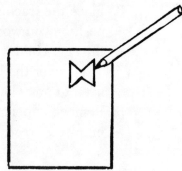

FELT

You can use the above method to transfer patterns to felt, or the following:

1. Place a thin piece of paper over the pattern in book. Trace over the lines using a pencil.

2. Cut out the paper patterns.

3. Place patterns on felt. With a pencil, trace around the paper patterns.

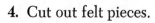

4. Cut out felt pieces.

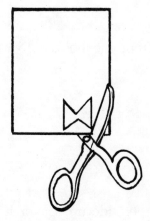

Household Decorations

Parrot Mosaic

If you have not worked with eggshells before and are wondering where to begin, try this easy parrot eggshell mosaic first. A piece of black cotton fabric was used for the background to create a needed contrast for the brilliant primary colors of the parrot. White and pastel colors are not as effective for the background as a primary color or black. The parrot mosaic will be a cheerful addition to any bedroom or game room wall.

What You Need

Materials

1 dozen broken eggshells
black cotton fabric, 13 by 16 inches
cardboard rectangle, 9 by 12 inches
glue
1 sheet tracing paper
acrylic paints
heavy string
brown paper tape

Tools

pencil
ruler
paintbrush
scissors
knife

Covering the Cardboard

1. With a knife, cut a piece of cardboard that is free from bends, holes, and dirt to 9 by 12 inches. Cut the sides straight and cut corners at right angles.
2. Steam press fabric to remove wrinkles and folds. Place cardboard in center of fabric, so that the fabric extends about 2 inches on all sides. Apply glue on back of cardboard along all four sides. Pulling the fabric tightly as you

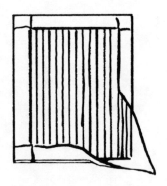

work, glue it to the back of the cardboard sides, making box pleats in all the corners. Keep fabric in place with heavy books or weights until glue dries.

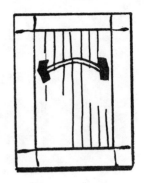

Attaching Hanger

1. Mark the back of the cardboard in two places, one-third down from the top and 1½ inches from the right. Repeat on the left. Cut two lengths of string 2 inches longer than the distance between the marks or, in this case, 8 inches long.

    Place the strings between the marks and line up the tips.

2. Cut two pieces of brown wrapping tape 4 inches long. Lick the tape and stick it over the ends of string to secure the string to the cardboard. When you complete the mosaic, hang the picture from the string on the wall.

Making the Mosaic

1. With white chalk, trace and transfer the parrot from design section in back of book to the fabric-covered cardboard. Lightly brush any residue of chalk from the fabric.

2. Break eggshells into large pieces to make them easy to paint. Paint eggshells in three or more colors using acrylic paints.

3. With a finger, apply glue to one area of the parrot design on the fabric. Place a piece of broken eggshell on the glue, paint side up. Press down on the eggshell until it cracks into small pieces. Continue gluing and pressing in

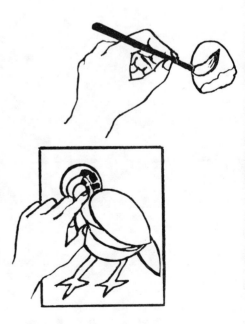

eggshell pieces until the design is complete. Use different colors of eggshell pieces for the various parts of the parrot. Let dry overnight.

There is also a fish pattern in the design section of the book which you can use for this project. All the steps are the same.

Mouse Mobile

White, round eggs resembling mice hop through the air suspended from a wire hanger and clear fishing line. The beautiful shape of the eggs makes a lovely decoration for a porch, family room, or above a crib. This one hangs from a macramé plant hanger that complements a dangling Boston fern above it.

The cost and time to make this mobile is very minimal. A medium-size steel wire is used for the hanger. The wire from a clothes hanger is too heavy to bend easily and would look too heavy in contrast to the delicate eggs.

What You Need

Materials

5 raw eggs
clear fishing line
steel wire
shellac
acrylic paints (red, black)
rubbing alcohol
paper plate
5 pieces of straw from a broom

Tools

scissors
paintbrush
wire cutters
1½-inch needle

Making a Mouse

1. Hollow out an egg.
2. Paint one eye on each side of a narrow end of egg using a small paintbrush and black acrylic paint. Let dry. Paint a mouth between the eyes in red acrylic paint. Let dry.
3. Repeat steps 1 and 2 with 4 more eggs.
4. Paint all the mice with shellac to harden the

shell and give the mice a more finished appearance. Let dry on paper plate. Clean brush out with rubbing alcohol.

5. Break a piece of broom straw into 6 pieces for whiskers. Glue straw pieces one by one above mouth. Repeat making whiskers and gluing them on the other 4 mice.

Making a Hanger
1. With a wire cutter, cut 2 pieces of wire—one 13 inches long, the other 9 inches long.

2. Bend the longer wire into a wide arch. Bend the shorter wire in a similar arch. Bend and twist both ends of each wire into small circles about ¼ inch in diameter. With wire cutter, cut off excess wire at circles.

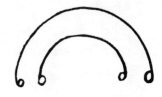

3. With scissors, cut a piece of fishing line 7 inches long. Attach the wires with the line, tying each end of the line to the center of each wire. Secure line with a knot.
4. You will need a loop at the top of hanger, so it will hang. Cut a piece of fishing line 8 inches

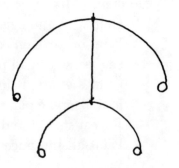

long. Bend the line in half. Place line at the center of the long wire, on the bend in line. Wind the line once around wire and secure it with a knot. Tie the remaining 2 loose ends of line in a secure knot. Using scissors, cut off any excess line.

Hanging the Mice

1. Each mouse should hang at a different level. Cut 5 pieces of fishing line in the following lengths: 3½ inches, 7½ inches, 8½ inches, 9½ inches, and 10½ inches.
2. Thread the 3½-inch line through a needle and tie a knot at the end of it. Put the needle through the center bottom of a mouse and push it out through the top. Unthread needle and tie the free end of line around the center of the short wire arch. Secure with a tight knot.
3. Repeat step 2 for the other 4 mice, using a different length of line for each mouse. Place the hanger flat on a table before tying the mice to it. Below is a guide to show you where each mouse should be tied. Secure each line with a tight knot.
   a. 10½-inch line on the right circle of long wire arch.
   b. 9½-inch line on the right circle of short wire arch.
   c. 8½-inch line on the left circle of long wire arch.
   d. 7½-inch line on the left circle of short wire arch.

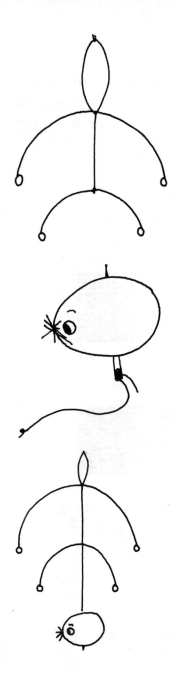

27

4. Hang the mobile by the loop at the top of the hanger from the ceiling or anywhere else it might catch a gust of wind.

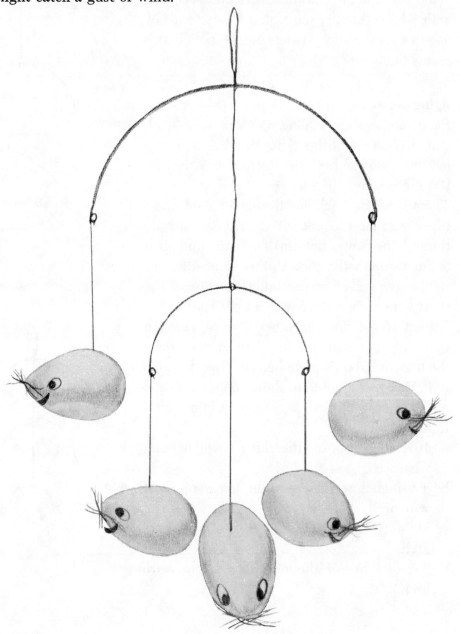

Abstract Wall Hanging

This project is sure to muster up the sometimes hidden creative instincts that lie within all people. It's fun to move the plaster-filled egg shapes in different positions and groups until a pleasing design for an abstract wall hanging is reached. At least a dozen or more hollow eggshells are required. When the wall hanging is done and on the wall, shine a direct light on it from different angles to see the wonderful patterns the shadows of the eggs create.

One thing you might want to do is paint the shapes in a variety of brilliant colors with acrylic paints. However, this one was left plain white and is very effective. The recipe below for the plaster of paris will fill 8 half-shells. The quantity of the plaster mix is fairly small to give you enough time to fill the shell shapes before the plaster sets. You will need to make two or more batches of plaster of paris, depending on the number of egg shapes you use to make the wall hanging.

What You Need

Materials

1–2 dozen eggs
2 cups plaster of paris
1 cup plus 2 tablespoons water
empty can
white acrylic paint
3 sheets medium sandpaper
2 empty egg cartons
1 sheet plywood board at least 12 by 12
    inches
2 metal hangers and screws
wire
(optional) many colors of acrylic paints

Tools

pencil
elastic band
paintbrush (optional)
screwdriver

Making Eggshell Shapes

1. Hollow out 12–24 eggs.
2. Break the hollow eggs in a variety of the following shapes.

   a. Short half-shells. Place an elastic band horizontally around the center of a hollow egg. Use the elastic as your guide and draw a line around the egg. Remove elastic. Carefully break off one end of the eggshell to the center line.

   b. Long half-shell. Place the elastic band vertically around a hollow egg. Draw a line around the egg. Remove elastic. Carefully break off one side of the eggshell to the line.

   c. Less than half. Smaller pieces or shapes that resemble half-shells can be made by breaking the hollow eggshells off a little more than half.

   d. Round wedge. Place an elastic band vertically around the center of a hollow egg. Draw a line around egg. Place the elastic horizontally around the center of the same hollow egg. Draw a line around the egg using a pencil. Remove elastic. The two lines should equally divide the egg into fourths. Carefully break ¾ of the eggshell off to leave a wedge-shaped piece. To vary the size of the wedge shape move the horizontal line lower or higher than the center of a hollow egg.

Perhaps you will come up with more ways to divide the egg into shapes. If so, try them!

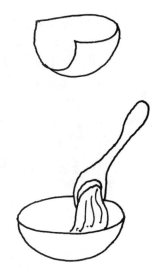

3. Mix 2 cups plaster of paris with 1 cup plus 2 tablespoons water in an empty can. Spoon the plaster into all eggshell shapes except the wedge. If the plaster is too thin to mold in the wedge shapes, then let it sit in the can until it begins to set. When the consistency resembles a soft clay it is ready for molding. Fill the wedge-shaped shells by molding the plaster in them with your hands, making a right angle where the sides meet. Place all shapes in an empty egg carton and let dry for 2 days.

4. Repeat step 3 until you have 12–24 plaster-filled egg shapes.

5. Spread 2 sheets of newspaper on a table or a hard, flat surface. Place a sheet of sandpaper on the newspapers. Sand all the plaster sides of the eggshell shapes by rubbing them back and forth on the sandpaper until they are smooth and flat. Use a new sheet of sandpaper as necessary.

Preparing the Board

1. Paint the top and sides of a plywood board with white acrylic paint, using a flat nylon brush. Use a thick coat of paint to cover the wood completely. Let dry.

2. Turn the board back side up. Measure and

mark in two places: 4 inches down from the top and 3 inches in from the right side. Repeat on the left side of board.

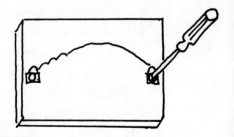

3. Screw the metal hangers in place on the two marks with screws and a screwdriver.

4. Measure the distance between the two hangers. Cut a length of wire 2 inches longer than the distance. Wrap the ends of wire around the metal hangers.

Finishing the Wall Hanging

1. (optional) Paint the eggshell shapes in a variety of colors, using acrylic paints and a brush. Let dry.

2. Place the painted plywood board in front of you on a table. Place all the plaster-filled shapes on board. Move the pieces around to make different combinations of shapes and compositions. When you like a set of forms together, leave them in place and either build around them with more shapes or begin new combinations of forms in another area of the board.

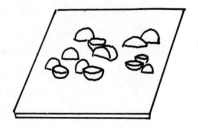

3. When you are finally pleased with a composition, then glue each shape individually in place, using white glue. Apply glue to either edge or the round bottom of an eggshell shape. Put it on board in place and hold for a few seconds. Glue all the shapes in place. Let the wall hanging dry overnight in a horizontal position.

4. Hang the wall hanging from the wire on a nail or picture hanger.

Gifts

Herb Pots

An attractive set of herb pots to be hung from an old gnarled branch can be made easily and makes a wonderful gift for someone.

Painting the design on the pots will take a little patience if you have not painted before, but the results will be very satisfying. If you are handy at making macramé plant hangers, then you might want to replace the simple yarn hangers called for here with more complicated macramé hangers. Make the macramé hangers fairly simple, for too much detail could overwhelm the small eggshell pots.

Some common herbs to grow in the pots are thyme, rosemary, parsley, mint, chives, basil, and marjoram.

What You Need

Materials

5 raw eggs
1 branch or piece of driftwood,
    18–20 inches long
1 cup plaster of paris
½ cup plus 1 tablespoon water
empty soup or coffee can
1 sheet medium sandpaper
rubbing alcohol
shellac
empty egg carton
yarn or thin macramé string

Tools

flat nylon brush
small round paintbrush
knife
scissors
pencil
ruler
wide elastic band

Making an Herb Pot

1. Hollow out an egg.
2. Mark the center of egg. Place a wide elastic band horizontally around the center at mark, and with a pencil draw a line around egg, using

the elastic as your guide. Start at the narrow end of egg and gently break off eggshell to the center line. Repeat steps 1 and 2 with the other 4 eggs.

3. Mix 1 cup plaster of paris with ½ cup plus 1 tablespoon of water in an empty can. Using the flat nylon brush, paint the inside walls of the 5 eggshells with plaster of paris about ¹⁄₁₆ inch thick.

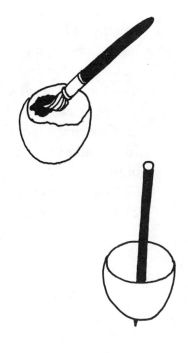

4. With the pointed end of a pencil, poke a hole through the plaster and the bottom of eggshell pot. This hole will provide proper drainage for the herb plant. Poke holes in remaining eggshells. Place all shells in an empty egg carton. Let dry overnight.

5. Place a piece of medium sandpaper on a hard, flat surface. Put each pot round side up on the sandpaper. Rub each back and forth until the jagged edges are flat and smooth.

Painting a Pot

1. Trace and transfer a design from the design section of book to the sides of a pot.

2. Paint in several colors with acrylic paints. Let dry. Use a clean brush to paint the entire outside of each pot with shellac. Let dry. Clean brush with rubbing alcohol.

Making a Hanger

1. If you do not have access to an old gnarled branch or a piece of driftwood 18–20 inches long, a wood dowel ½ inch in diameter will work out very well.

2. Cut 4 pieces of yarn in each of the following

lengths: 18 inches, 24 inches, 28 inches, 30 inches, and 36 inches.

3. Take the four 18-inch pieces of yarn, smooth them against each other, and line the tips together. Make a large knot at each end. Tie another knot 8 inches away from the first knot. In the same way tie 3 knots in the other lengths of yarn.

4. Slide each yarn hanger over the branch so that 2 knotted strings hang on one side of the branch and 2 on the other side. Here is an example of the order in which to hang the yarn hangers. First the 30-inch, then 24-inch, 36-inch, 28-inch, and finally the 18-inch hanger.

5. Cut 2 pieces of yarn 2 feet long. Smooth them against each other and line up the tips. Loop one end of the yarn around the right side of the branch. Tie in a tight double knot. Tie the other end on the left side of branch. Secure with a tight double knot. With scissors cut off any excess yarn at the knots.

6. Hang the branch by this top piece of yarn on a hook or nail in the wall, above or near a sunny window.

7. Place each pot on the bottom knot of each yarn hanger. Separate the yarn of each hanger, so that the four strands are evenly spaced around a pot.

8. Here is a list of various herbs you can grow in the herb pots, with the instructions for growing them and their uses.
Basil: Needs full sun and warm soil. Water it

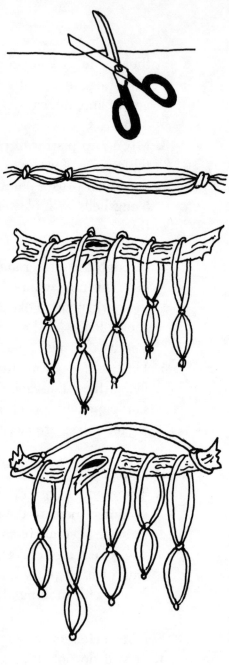

regularly. Use fresh or dried leaves in salads, sauces, and vegetable dishes.

Chives: Like moist soil and lots of sunlight. Use cut strands for a mild onion flavor in salads, soups, and with cheeses.

Dill: Needs full sun, average soil. Fresh or dried dill is used in salads, meat dishes, and sauces.

Mint: Best growth is in light, moist soil in part shade. Use fresh mint leaves as a garnish or in cold drinks. Fresh or dried leaves in cooking, especially with lamb.

Oregano: Needs full sun, moderate watering. Fresh or dried leaves are used in many dishes and sauces, especially Spanish and Italian.

Parsley: Will tolerate various growing conditions but grows best in full sun and fairly moist soil. Use fresh or dried leaves in salads, vegetable dishes, and sauces.

Thyme: Needs well-drained and fairly dry soil in full sun. The fresh or dried leaves are used in preparing meats, fish, poultry, vegetables and sauces.

A potting soil with humus or peat moss is recommended for potting herbs. Both substances hold moisture in the soil. Most potting soils sold commercially contain either or both of these materials.

Organizer Tray

Paper clips, stamps, stickers, erasers, pen cartridges, safety pins, buttons, earrings, necklaces, or anything small that clutters a desk or dresser can be organized in this tray. It not only serves as an organizer but adds a personal touch to a dresser or desk.

The person you make it for and the purpose it serves should dictate the design and colors you decide to use.

What You Need

Materials

6 raw eggs
1 cup plaster of paris
½ cup plus 1 tablespoon water
empty soup or coffee can
acrylic paints
shellac
rubbing alcohol
sheet of medium sandpaper
glue

Tools

pencil
ruler
flat nylon brush, 1 inch wide
small round paintbrush
wide elastic band

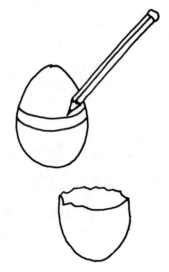

Making a Tray

1. Hollow out 6 raw eggs.
2. Mark the center of each hollow eggshell. Place an elastic band horizontally around the center at mark, and with a pencil draw a line around egg, using the elastic as your guide. Remove elastic. Repeat on other 5 eggs.
3. Start at the narrow end of egg and carefully break each eggshell evenly down to the center line.

4. Mix 1 cup plaster of paris with ½ cup plus 1 tablespoon of water in an empty can. Paint the plaster of paris on the inside walls of all half-shells about ⅟₁₆ inch thick, using a flat nylon brush. Let dry overnight in an empty egg carton.

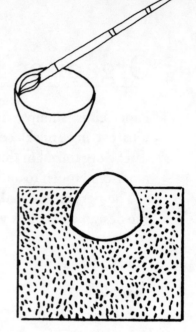

5. Place a piece of medium sandpaper on a hard, flat surface. Put each half-shell round side up on the sandpaper and gently rub it back and forth until edges are flat and smooth.

Assembling the Tray

1. Apply a dot of glue on the outside of 2 half-shells, ¼ inch down from the top flat edge. Put the two shells together at glue point and hold for a minute. Turn them flat side down on a table and let dry overnight. Repeat with the other 4 half-shells to make two more sets.

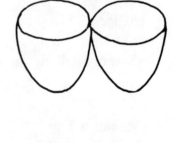

2. Glue together, as above, two sets of half-shells to form a square. Glue the remaining set on one end of the square to create a rectangular tray of half-shells. Let dry overnight.

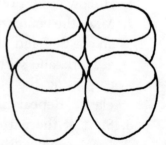

Finishing the Tray

1. Trace and transfer a design from the design section of book to the side of each half-shell.
2. Paint in the design with acrylic paints, using a small round paintbrush. Let dry. It should dry in a matter of minutes.
3. Using a clean paintbrush, paint the entire tray with shellac. Let dry. Clean out brush with rubbing alcohol.

Candlestick Holders

These pretty candlestick holders cost only a few cents to make if you have a paintbrush and sandpaper around the house. They look simple, elegant, modern, whether left plain white or painted a solid color. One way to make them personal and unique is to paint your own designs on them or trace a design from the book and paint it.

What You Need

Materials

2 raw eggs
1 cup plaster of paris
½ cup water
paper tube found inside of wrapping
   paper
1 inch wide masking tape
1 sheet medium sandpaper
candles
tracing paper

Tools

pencil
ruler
scissors
knife
flat nylon brush, 1 inch wide
   or spoon

Making Candlestick Holders

1. Hollow out 2 raw eggs.
2. Trace and transfer the circle at the right in the book to the wide end of the hollow eggs. Remove the eggshell from the inside of circle with thumb and forefinger to make a hole for the candlestick. Slowly sand edges of hole smooth with a small piece of sandpaper.
3. Make a pencil mark ½ inch from the narrow end of both hollow eggs. Break the eggshells off evenly to mark.

4. Take paper tube and mark 1 inch off. Place tube on a cutting board. Holding it with one hand, cut through the tube at mark with a knife. Repeat to make another 1 inch wide paper ring.

5. To make a mold for holding the candlesticks in holders, cut each ring with scissors. Wrap one ring around the bottom of a candle, overlapping the ends of ring in order to make the correct size for a candle. Hold ring in place. Tape ring together with masking tape. Slide it off the candle. Repeat, taping other ring. Cover one open end of each ring with masking tape.

6. Fit one cardboard ring inside a hollow egg, so that its top is even with the edge of egg and the masking-taped end of ring is inside of eggshell candlestick holder.

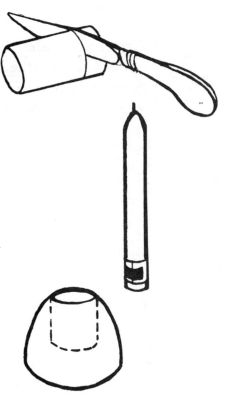

7. Mix 1 cup plaster of paris with ½ cup water in an empty can. The consistency should be thick like clay. Turn the candlestick holders upside down. Using a nylon brush or spoon, fill each holder with plaster around the cardboard rings. In twenty minutes remove the cardboard rings from the inside of the candlestick holders through the top hole. Discard rings. Let dry overnight.

8. Place a piece of medium sandpaper on a hard, flat surface. Place each candlestick holder upside down on the sandpaper and gently rub back and forth until top edges are smooth and flat. Sand the bottom of each holder in the same way.

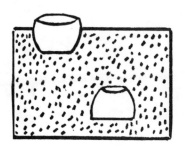

9. Trace and transfer a design from the design section of book to the holders.
10. Put a candle in each holder.

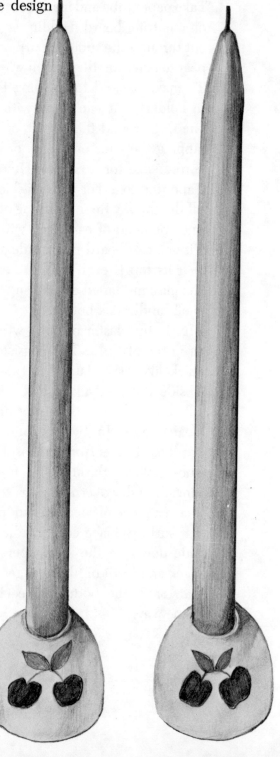

Necklace

You can make an eggshell necklace that looks like the hand-painted porcelain necklaces sold today. It is inexpensive and easy to make, especially if painting is not hard for you. One advantage this necklace has over the porcelain type is that it is much more durable because it is filled with plaster of paris. You might want to make several while you are at it. If so, then double or triple the plaster of paris recipe and hollow out an egg for each necklace.

The sample designs in the back of the book were painted in one color, but you can certainly make yours as colorful as you like.

What You Need

Materials

1 raw egg
½ cup plaster of paris
¼ cup plus 1 tablespoon water
an empty soup or coffee can
shellac
rubbing alcohol
2 feet smooth nylon macramé string
empty egg carton
small wooden beads (optional)
1 sheet medium sandpaper
tracing paper

Tools

flat nylon brush, 1 inch wide,
  or a spoon
wide elastic band
pencil
small round paintbrush
scissors

Making a Necklace

1. Hollow out an egg.
2. Place a wide elastic band vertically around a hollow egg. Using the elastic as a guide, draw a line around egg. Remove elastic.
3. Carefully break off ½ of the eggshell to the

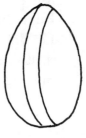

line so that a long half-shell remains for the necklace.

4. With scissors, cut a piece of smooth nylon macramé string 2 feet long.

5. Mix ½ cup plaster of paris and ¼ cup plus 1 tablespoon of water in an empty can. Fill the half-eggshell ¾ full with plaster, using the nylon brush or a spoon. Place the nylon string across the center of plaster-filled eggshell. Make certain there are equal lengths of string on each side of the necklace. Fill the remaining space in necklace with plaster of paris covering the nylon string. Place in empty egg carton. Let dry overnight.

6. Place a sheet of sandpaper on a hard, flat surface. Put necklace plaster side down on sandpaper, and rub it back and forth until plaster is smooth and flat.

7. Trace and transfer a necklace design from the design section of book to the round side of the necklace. Paint in the design with acrylic paint, using a small round paintbrush. Let dry.

8. Paint the back of the necklace with shellac. Let dry. Paint the round decorative side with shellac. Let dry. Clean out shellac brush with rubbing alcohol.

9. (Optional) String beads on each side of the necklace.

Eggshell and Tissue Flowers

These bright tissue flowers will add a festive spark of color to any room. Once you find out how easy they are to make, you might want to make them for all your friends and relatives as gifts.

Use at least two shades of a color for each flower to create depth and variety. One possibility is yellow with a reddish orange center for the daisy, blues for the chrysanthemum, pink and violet for the rose, and yellow and orange for the daffodil.

What You Need

Materials

4 raw eggs
8 pieces of colored tissue,
    18 by 18 inches
1 piece of green tissue or
    crepe paper for leaves
thin cardboard
wire for stems—medium weight
green floral tape
glue
tracing paper

Tools

scissors
pencil
ruler

Making a Chrysanthemum

1. Hollow out an egg.
2. Trace the chrysanthemum petal from the design section of book and transfer it to a thin piece of cardboard. Cut out petal with scissors.
3. Place a light shade of tissue paper on a dark shade of tissue paper. Mark off 2 inches from the bottom. Fold both sheets at mark. Place the cardboard petal on the folded tissue, flat

end just above the fold. Trace around the petal 20 times in a row. With scissors, starting at the top of the fold, cut out tissue petals. Do not cut through the fold. You should have a long strip of petals attached at the fold.

4. Mark off 1 inch down from the wide end of hollow egg.

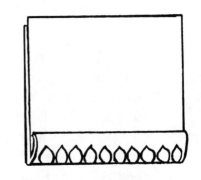

5. Put a line of glue on tissue strip just below the petals. Starting at the mark on the egg, wind the petals around the egg several times. Glue each row just above the last yet as close to each other as possible. Bend each petal outward to create a fluffy chrysanthemum.

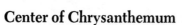

Center of Chrysanthemum

1. Cut a piece of the lighter shade of tissue you used about 9 inches wide and 6 inches high. Fold it horizontally in half 3 times.

2. With scissors, make cuts in the folded tissue about 1⁄16 inch apart down to the fold but not through it. This will be the center of the flower.

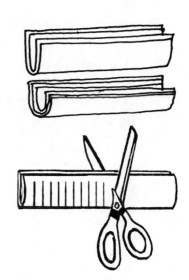

Glue the strip of tissue just above the petals in a circle.

3. Cut a piece of the darker shade of tissue 3 inches by 3 inches. Glue it on the bottom of the flower below the petals. Fold and apply glue whenever necessary to completely cover the eggshell with tissue.

Making a Rose

1. Hollow out an egg.
2. Trace and transfer the 3 different sizes of rose petals from the design section of book to a thin piece of cardboard. Cut out cardboard petals.
3. Mark 1 inch from the bottom of a dark shade of tissue. Fold tissue at mark.
4. Place the large cardboard petal on tissue just above the fold. Trace around it 12 times in a row. Cut out the petals without cutting through the fold.
5. Mark 1 inch down from the wide end of hollow egg.
6. Place a line of glue below tissue petals, at the fold. Start gluing the petals at mark then proceed to wind them around the egg several times. Glue each row above the last row, as close to each other as possible.
7. Mark 1 inch from the bottom of a light shade of tissue paper. Fold at mark. Trace the medium and small petals 8 times in a row just above the fold and cut them out without cutting through the fold.
8. Glue them to the egg in the same manner as step 6. Glue the medium petals above the large

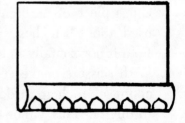

petals and finally glue the small petals in a circle in the center of the rose. Slightly bend each petal out from the eggshell.

Making a Daisy

1. Hollow out an egg.
2. Trace and transfer the daisy petal from the design section of book to a thin piece of cardboard. Cut out cardboard petal.
3. Mark 4 inches from the bottom of a sheet of tissue. Fold at mark. Place the flat end of cardboard petal on the fold and trace around it 8 times in a row. Using scissors, cut out each double-thick petal. This time *do* cut through the fold.

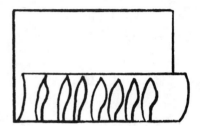

4. Take one double-thick petal and fold the top petal at an angle to the bottom petal so that the petals face each other. Repeat with other 7 petals.

5. Mark 1 inch down from the wide end of the hollow egg. Glue the daisy petals in a circle around the egg at the level of the mark.

Center of Daisy

1. Cut out a piece of tissue 9 inches wide and 6 inches high. Fold it horizontally in half 2 times.
2. Make cuts about $\frac{1}{16}$ inch apart down to the fold but not through it.
3. Place a line of glue on the tissue above the fold. Glue center in a circle just above the petals.
4. Cut a piece of tissue that measures 3 inches by 3 inches. Glue it to the bottom of the daisy. Fold and apply glue whenever necessary to cover the eggshell completely.

Making a Daffodil

1. Hollow out an egg.
2. Trace and transfer the daffodil petal from the design section of book to a thin piece of cardboard. Cut out petal.
3. Mark 4 inches from the bottom of a piece of tissue. Fold at mark. Fold again, so that there are 3 layers of tissue 4 inches high.
4. Place the cardboard petal on the bottom fold of tissue. Trace around it 6 times in a row. Cut out each petal. You should have 5 separate petals 3 layers thick.
5. Mark 1 inch from the wide end of the hollow egg.
6. Glue the petals around the egg in a circle at the level of mark.

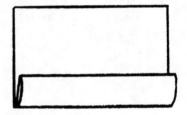

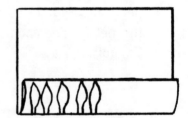

Center of Daffodil

1. Cut a piece of tissue 9 inches long and 4 inches high. Fold in half horizontally.
2. Cut the top edge of tissue in round zigzags like a trail of a snake.
3. Place a line of glue just above fold and glue the center in a circle above the petals. It should look like a 2 inch high tube that tilts inward. Make cuts in the tissue center ½ inch apart and ¾ inch long. Slightly bend out center of the daffodil.
4. Cut a piece of tissue in the same color as the petals 3 inches by 3 inches. Glue it to the bottom of the daffodil. Fold tissue and apply glue wherever necessary to completely cover eggshell with tissue.

Attaching Stem and Leaves to Flower

1. With wire cutters, cut a piece of wire 12 inches long.
2. Mark 1 inch from an end of the wire. Bend wire at mark in a right angle.
3. Apply glue on the bent part of wire. Stick wire through the bottom hole of eggshell flower. Prop wire stem against the inside top of eggshell for a minute, so that it will adhere to the eggshell flower.
4. Cut a piece of floral tape about 12 inches long. Glue one end of tape to the bottom of eggshell flower next to the wire stem. Let dry.

5. Cut several leaves out of green tissue or crepe paper. Crease the middle of each leaf to make it more rigid.

6. Wind the floral tape around the wire stem very tightly. Place a leaf against the stem every so often and secure it to the stem by winding the floral tape around the bottom of leaf. The floral tape is sticky and will not come unwound. Completely cover stem with floral tape.

7. Attach stems and leaves to all flowers. Place flowers in a vase.

Decorated Eggs

Here is an inexpensive way to make a beautiful gift for someone. The painted eggs can be displayed all year round on a coffee table or in a corner cabinet. See the design section at the back of the book for suggested designs. Acrylic paints are ideal to paint the eggs. Tube watercolor paints also work very well, provided a coat of shellac is applied over the watercolor when dry. Various items may be used as stands for the eggs: napkin rings, drawer pulls, a 2 ounce glass measure, or a small woven basket sold at arts and crafts supply stores.

What You Need

Materials

1 raw egg
acrylic or watercolor tube paints—
    several colors
shellac
rubbing alcohol
thin tracing paper
carbon paper
scrap of cardboard or a paper plate

Tools

pencil
small round paintbrush

Valentine Eggs

1. Hollow out an egg.
2. Place a piece of tracing paper on a design in the design section of book and trace over it.
3. Place a sheet of carbon paper under tracing paper, ink side down. Place both sheets on egg, ink side against egg, and trace over the design with a pencil. Turn egg to clean side and trace the design on it in the same manner, so that a continuous design around the entire egg is achieved. Remove papers.

4. On a scrap of cardboard put a dab of each color of acrylic or watercolor paint you intend to use.
5. With the paintbrush, paint the middle of the egg first, and then each end. Doing it this way allows you to hold the egg by both ends as you paint. Use any colors. Let dry.
6. (optional) Paint the entire egg with shellac to give it a more finished appearance. Let dry. Clean brush with rubbing alcohol.
7. Place painted egg in stand such as those mentioned above.

Birthday Eggs
1. Repeat steps 1–7 of the Valentine Eggs, using the birthday designs.

Easter Eggs
1. Repeat steps 1–7 of the Valentine Eggs, using the Easter designs.

Christmas Eggs
1. Repeat steps 1–7 of Valentine Eggs, using the Christmas designs.

Christmas Decorations

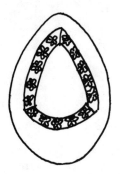

Ribbon Mobile

Hang this intriguing mobile at your front door to welcome visiting relatives or friends during the Christmas holidays. You might want to hang a bit of fresh holly or mistletoe from the bottom of the mobile.

The type of ribbon you use to cover the eggs will determine the character of the mobile. Try to use ribbons with at least 6 different designs.

What You Need

Materials

6 raw eggs
6–8 feet ribbon not wider than ¾ inch
2 feet heavy yarn or macramé string
   in red or green
1 yard medium steel wire
   clear fishing line

Tools

scissors
pencil
ruler
wire cutter
embroidery needle

Covering Eggs with Ribbon

1. Hollow out 6 raw eggs.
2. You can cover each egg with 1 vertical and 1 horizontal ribbon, or with 2 vertical pieces of ribbon. To measure the ribbon for the egg, wrap it completely around the egg vertically. Mark the spot and cut the ribbon. Repeat around the center of the egg.
3. Apply glue to the back of ribbon and glue it vertically around the egg. Smooth down the edges of the ribbon. Press down on the 2 ends of ribbon until dry. Cover all 6 eggs with 2 pieces of ribbon in the method described above. Let dry.

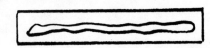

Making a Hanger

1. Cut 3 pieces of wire in the following lengths: 9½ inches, 11½ inches, and 12½ inches.
2. Mark 2 inches from the end of one wire. Bend at mark in a right angle. Repeat on opposite end of wire. Bend the ends of the other 2 wires in the same way.
3. Using the wire cutter, twist all bent ends into tiny circles. Cut excess wire from circles with the wire cutter.
4. Take 2 feet of yarn. Wrap one end of it around the center of shortest wire. Secure with a knot. Tie the medium wire 5 inches above the center of the shortest wire by securing it with a knot. Tie the remaining long wire 6 inches above the middle wire by tying a secure knot in the center of the wire.
5. Measure 4 inches from the tip of yarn and make a loop. Tie the tip of yarn at the mark in a secure knot. This is the hanger.

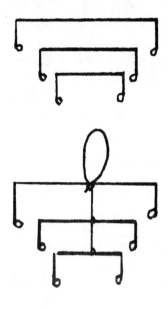

Attaching Eggs to Hanger

1. With scissors, cut 6 pieces of fishing line: 2 pieces 10 inches long and 4 pieces 8 inches long.
2. Thread one 10-inch line through the eye of a needle. Tie a knot at the opposite end of line. Gently push needle all the way through the egg, starting at the center bottom of the egg. Then push the tip of the needle through the center top of the egg firmly but gently. Unthread needle. Tie the free end of the line to a circle on the longest wire. Secure with a knot.

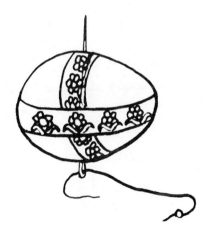

Repeat with the second 10-inch line and second ribbon-covered egg. Tie this one on the opposite circle. Secure with a knot.

3. Attach the remaining 4 eggs to the circles on the other two wires, using the 8-inch pieces of fishing line. Secure each with a knot.

Christmas Scene in an Egg

Here is an easy way to make your own special Christmas tree ornaments. It takes just a few materials and a little bit of time to make a Christmas scene in an egg that will add home made charm to your tree for years.

The miniatures in the ornament should not be larger than 1¼ inches high or they will not fit into the egg.

What You Need

Materials

1 raw egg
1½ feet of ½ inch wide ribbon, embroidered in red or green, or satin ribbon
½ cup plaster of paris
¼ cup plus 1 tablespoon water
plastic or wood miniatures—snowman, elves, etc.
empty soup or coffee can
empty egg carton

Tools

pencil
wide elastic band
scissors
flat nylon brush, 1 inch wide

Making an Ornament

1. Hollow out an egg.
2. To make an arched opening, place an elastic band vertically around egg. Using this as a guide, draw a line from top to bottom of egg. Move the elastic about 1¼ inches to the right of the line and draw another vertical line from top to bottom. Remove elastic. Mark off ½ inch from bottom wide end of egg. Draw a

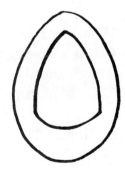

horizontal line connecting the two vertical lines at mark. With thumb and forefinger, carefully remove the eggshell between the vertical and horizontal lines.

3. Mix ½ cup plaster of paris with ¼ cup plus 1 tablespoon of water in an empty can. With nylon brush, paint the inside of the eggshell with plaster. Fill the bottom of the eggshell with plaster up to the opening, using a brush or spoon. Level the plaster as flat as possible. Place egg in empty egg carton. Let dry overnight.

4. To measure the ribbon that outlines the opening, place a ribbon along the right edge of opening. Mark the distance from top to bottom on ribbon. Cut ribbon at marks. Apply glue to back of ribbon. Place it along the right edge and gently press into place. Let dry. Repeat measuring, cutting, and gluing ribbon on the left and bottom of opening. Let dry.

5. Glue 2 or 3 miniatures inside the egg on the plaster. Apply a dab of glue to the bottom of each miniature. Hold miniature in place for a minute until it can stand up straight by itself.

Making a Hanger

1. Cut a piece of ribbon 8 inches long. Tie the ends together to form a knot. Pierce the top of the eggshell and plaster with the end of a scissor blade to make a hole.

2. Thread the loop of ribbon opposite the knot

through the hole, so that the knot remains on the inside of the ornament.

3. Hang ornament on tree by loop of ribbon.

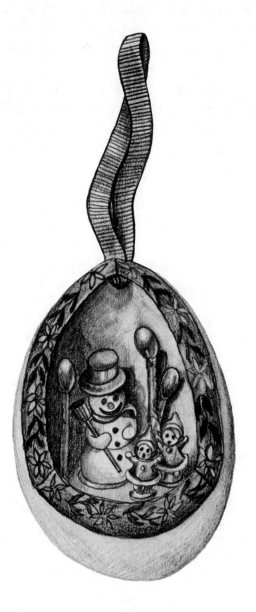

Standing Angel Decoration

A perfect project for a cold, snowy day before Christmas is this endearing angel. The time spent on making her will be well worth the effort. The beautiful results will add a special touch to a Christmas centerpiece or mantel display.

Choose fabric and embroidered ribbon in red and green for the angel's robe. If you can't find embroidered ribbon in your area, plaids or plain satin ribbon will be just as pretty. The ribbon should not be any wider than ¾ inch. Thinner ribbon, ½ inch wide, is easiest to use.

What You Need

Materials

1 raw egg
¼ yard fabric—red check
   or a small print
thin cardboard
3 yards ribbon in a variety of colors
1½ feet white eyelet trim
1 6-inch styrofoam cone
glue
red felt
straight pins
plastic or wire rod to attach head
   to styrofoam cone
toilet paper tube
acrylic paint or fine felt
   pens—for face
yellow embroidery thread—hair
tracing paper

Tools

pencil
ruler
knife
scissors
paintbrush or felt pens

Covering Angel Body

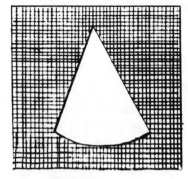

1. To make a pattern, trace the angel body from the design section of book onto a thin piece of paper. Cut out pattern. Place it on fabric. Trace around pattern with pencil and cut out pattern.

2. Wrap fabric around styrofoam cone so that ¼ inch of fabric is higher than the top of cone. Pin fabric in place with straight pins.

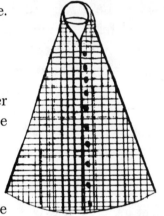

3. Overlap fabric at the top to completely cover cone. Pin in place with a straight pin. Pin the fabric underneath cone, using straight pins.

4. Cut 4 pieces of ribbon 6½ inches long. Glue each ribbon vertically to fabric-covered cone, spacing the ribbon evenly.

5. Cut pieces of ribbon in the following lengths: 9½ inches, 7½ inches, 6½ inches, 5¼ inches, and 4 inches.

6. Starting with the 9½-inch ribbon on the bottom, glue the ribbon horizontally around the cone. Add the 7½-inch a little higher up. Continue upward with the next longest length of ribbon, until the 4-inch ribbon is near the top of cone. Make sure the ends of the ribbon touch in back of the angel, so that the ribbons look like rings around the cone.

Wings

1. Trace and transfer the wing pattern from the design section of book onto a thin piece of cardboard. Cut out with scissors. Make another wing by tracing around the first wing and cut out the second cardboard wing.

2. Trace one cardboard wing 4 times on a piece of red felt. Cut out felt wings. Run a line of glue around the edge of one cardboard wing. Place a felt wing on top. Press in place. Turn the wing over and glue another felt wing to the back of the cardboard wing. Put a heavy book or heavy weight on the felt-covered cardboard wing and let dry.

3. Repeat step 2 to make another felt-covered cardboard wing.

4. Cut 6 pieces of eyelet trim each 3 inches long. Cut 12 pieces of ribbon each 3 inches long.

5. Glue 3 pieces of eyelet along the edges of one wing, overlapping the trim on the corners. Repeat on second wing. Place a heavy book or weight on the wings until they are dry.

6. Glue 3 pieces of ribbon to the front of one wing next to the eyelet trim, overlapping the ends at corners. Turn wing over and glue 3 more pieces of ribbon along the edges of wing, overlapping the ends at corners. Repeat on second wing using 6 more pieces of ribbon. Place both wings under a book or heavy weight. Let dry.

7. Mark 1½ inches down from the top of cone in the back. For the wings, use a knife to cut through the fabric-covered cone, making two

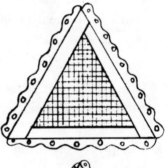

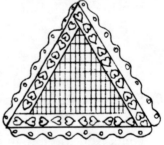

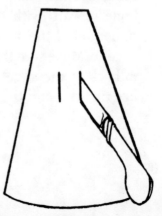

slots 1 inch apart from each other and about ½ inch long.

8. Apply glue to one corner of wing. Insert wing into a slot. Hold in position for a minute. Repeat with second wing. Let dry.

Collar

1. Trace the collar from the design section of book onto a thin piece of paper. Cut out paper collar. Place pattern on a piece of red felt. Trace pattern with a pencil. Cut out felt collar.
2. Wrap the collar around the top of the cone. Pin in place at the back of angel body with a straight pin.

Angel Head

1. Hollow out an egg.
2. If you are right-handed, hold your left thumb and forefinger about 2 inches apart. Wrap yellow embroidery thread around your fingers about 30 times. Carefully remove the thread from your fingers. Place the circle of thread on a table. With scissors, cut through all 30 strands.

3. Apply a layer of glue to the top and back of the wide end of a hollow egg. Place the thread hair on the egg evenly, so that it is 2 inches long on each side of the face. You will have to flatten the strands of thread to cover both sides and back of the head. Make bangs by gluing separate pieces of thread about ½ inch long on the front of head. Trim hair with scissors if necessary.

4. Draw in face with fine felt-tip pens or paint it

in with watercolors or acrylic paints and a small paintbrush. Use the final sketch of the angel as an example to draw or paint on face. Felt-tip pens might be easier to use than paint. If you make a mistake, you will be able to wipe it off with a damp paper towel.

Halo

1. Mark ½ inch from the end of a toilet paper tube. To cut with a knife, place tube on a cutting board, hold in place with one hand, and carefully cut through tube at mark.

2. Measure and cut a rectangle out of a thin piece of cardboard that is ½ inch wide and 2 inches long, using scissors.

3. Cut a piece of ½ inch wide ribbon 2 inches long. Glue ribbon to the 2-inch rectangle. Let dry.

4. Cut a piece of ½ inch wide ribbon 5 inches long. Place a line of glue on back of ribbon. Place ribbon around the outside of the ½-inch paper tube piece, so that the edges line up. Let dry.

5. Glue the cardboard rectangle to the paper tube halo, so that the top edge of the rectangle is flush with the top edge of the halo. Put a dab of glue on the back of the angel's head. Stick the rectangle on glue to make the halo rest just above the angel head. Hold in place until halo will stay on by itself. Let dry.

71

Painted Tree Ornaments

Make your Christmas tree a personal expression by painting hollow egg ornaments to hang on it. The designs at the back of the book will start you on your way to making beautiful ornaments that mass-produced types cannot possibly compete with. A good sable brush is needed for painting the designs on the eggs.

What You Need

Materials

1 raw egg
acrylic paints
gold ink
yarn or thin ribbon
scrap of cardboard
(optional)
shellac
rubbing alcohol
tracing paper
carbon paper

Tools

small paintbrush #2
scissors
3-inch needle
pencil

Making an Ornament

1. Hollow out an egg.
2. Trace a design from the design section of book onto a piece of tracing paper.
3. Place the tracing paper on a piece of carbon paper, ink side down, and place both sheets on the egg with the ink side against it.

4. Trace the design onto the egg, exerting a slight amount of pressure on pencil. The ornament with the candle, wreath, tree, and angel on it should have a different design on all 4 sides of the egg. You must trace 4 designs instead of the regular 2 designs on each side. The tree design is repeated 4 times on a single egg to achieve a continuous design too.

Painting the Ornament
1. Apply a dab of green, red, blue, silver, and black paint on a scrap of cardboard.
2. Paint one color at a time. Rinse the brush before using each new color. The consistency of the paint should be thick enough to cover the egg but thin enough to spread evenly.

Making a Hanger
1. Cut a piece of yarn or thin ribbon 8 inches long.

2. Thread the head of a needle with one end of yarn or ribbon. Tie the opposite end in a secure knot.

3. Insert the needle in the bottom hole of the egg and push it through the top hole. Unthread needle.

4. Make a loop of yarn or ribbon at the top of the ornament, tying the tip in a secure knot. Cut off any excess yarn or ribbon at knot.

5. Hang the ornament on Christmas tree by the yarn or ribbon loop.

Toys

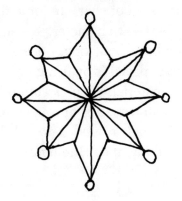

Puppets

You can make puppets out of hollow eggshells and felt that will hold up through all kinds of calamities if you fill the eggshells with plaster. No two puppets are ever alike. Yours will develop its own personality as you create it.

The following instructions for an eggshell puppet head and felt body can be the starting point for any kind of character or animal you choose to make, such as a favorite storybook character. Detailed instructions are also given for completing a bear, lion, king, queen, and bird.

One way to make the puppets special is by using lots of bright colors of felt in the bodies. Common materials such as cotton balls, pieces of carpeting, twine, fabric scraps, and macaroni might inspire ideas for puppet animals and characters. Look around. You will be surprised at the number of ideas you find lurking about the house.

What You Need

Materials	*Tools*
5 raw eggs	pencil
plaster of paris	ruler
¼ cup water	scissors
empty soup or coffee can	embroidery needle
embroidery thread or yarn	knife
wiggle eyes	
glue	
thin cardboard	
toilet paper tube	
2 pieces of felt, 10 by 10 inches	
tracing paper	

Making a Puppet Head

1. Hollow out an egg.
2. Mark ½ inch from the narrow end. Gradually break the narrow end of eggshell off evenly to mark.

3. Mix ½ cup plaster of paris with ¼ cup water in an empty can. With your hands, mold the plaster of paris into the hollow egg, leaving a deep finger hole in the center. Let dry overnight.

4. Mark ¾ inch from the end of a toilet paper tube. Place paper tube on a cutting board. Hold tube and with a knife carefully make a straight cut through it at the mark.

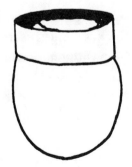

5. Apply a line of glue on the inside of the top edge of the cut piece of tube. Place it over the open end of the plaster-filled eggshell. Let dry overnight.

Making a Felt Puppet Body

1. Cut 2 pieces of felt 10 by 10 inches. Place one piece squarely on top of the other piece. Fold in half.

2. Trace the puppet body pattern from the design section of book onto tracing paper. Cut out pattern.

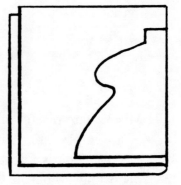

3. Place the straight edge of the body pattern on the fold of felt. Trace around the pattern. Holding the felt in place, cut out body. Unfold felt. If you are making the king or queen, cut off the rounded edges of the felt arms, so you have a straight line.

4. Cut a piece of embroidery thread or yarn 18 inches long. Insert thread into the needle, tie opposite end in a knot.

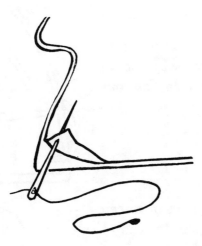

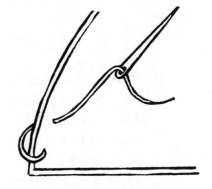

5. Sew the front and back body pieces of felt together in this way: Starting underneath and at the bottom of the left side of the body, stitch both pieces of felt together. Take the needle through the same hole again, making a loose circle. Slide the needle through the circle and pull thread tight. Take the needle underneath about ¼ inch from last stitch, slide it through the loop, pull the thread tight. Repeat, going up the left side until you reach the neck of felt

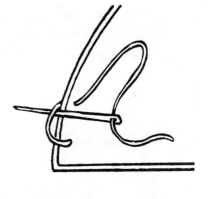

body pieces. Tie a secure knot. Sew the right side of the felt body in the same way. Leave the bottom of the puppet body open, for your hand.

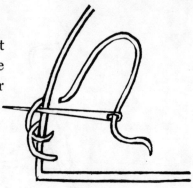

6. If you are sewing the body of king or queen puppets, leave the arm holes open. Instead of sewing the body up completely, tie a knot underneath the armhole, then continue sewing above armhole.

7. Apply a line of glue around the outside of the cardboard tube neck on the eggshell head. Insert the cardboard tube neck into felt neck pieces on body. Hold in place for a minute. Let dry.

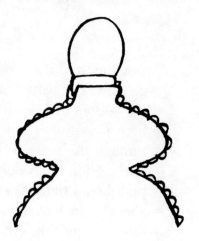

LION

What You Need

Materials
1 plaster-filled eggshell head
gold felt pieces, 10 by 10 inches
scraps of brown, green, red felt
2 wiggle eyes
fluff fiber—arts and crafts store
glue
embroidery thread or yarn
carbon paper
tracing paper

Tools
pencil
scissors
embroidery needle

Lion's Head

1. Trace and transfer the nose pattern from the design section of book onto a piece of thin cardboard. Cut out cardboard nose.
2. Bend cardboard nose where dotted lines are shown.
3. Trace the nose pieces from the design section of book onto a thin piece of paper. Cut out patterns. Trace around the patterns with a pencil onto the felt. Cut out felt nose pieces and glue them to cardboard nose. Let dry.

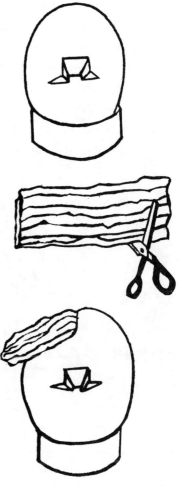

4. Glue the nose to a plaster-filled eggshell head. Hold down the sides of nose until they stay put by themselves. Let dry.

5. Cut off one end of fluff fiber about 1½ inches long.

6. Take a small quantity of the fiber. Flatten it. Apply a line of glue along one end and glue it to the top of the eggshell head. Continue flattening and gluing the fiber to head from top to bottom. Keep your hands free of glue or the fiber will stick to them instead of the eggshell head.

81

7. Glue 2 wiggle eyes on each side of nose. Let dry. Bits of felt cut to resemble eyes could be used in place of wiggle eyes.
8. Cut a piece of red felt in the shape of a mouth.

Lion's Body
1. With the 2 pieces of 10-inch-square felt pieces, make a body as described on page 78. Glue lion body to lion's head.
2. Trace the patterns for paws and a bow tie from the design section of book onto a piece of tracing paper. Cut out all patterns.
3. Place the paw patterns on green felt and the bow tie on red felt. Trace around the patterns; then cut out. Glue in place on the lion's body. Let dry.

BEAR

What You Need

Materials

1 plaster-filled eggshell head
2 pieces of brown felt, 10 by 10 inches
brown yarn
2 wiggle eyes
scraps of felt—light blue, tan, gold,
   dark brown, red
embroidery thread or yarn
glue
tracing paper

Tools

pencil
scissors
embroidery needle

Bear's Head

1. Smear a layer of glue on the top half of a plaster-filled eggshell head.
2. Starting at the top of head glue brown yarn in circular rows around the head until it is completely covered. Let dry.
3. Cut out a circle of gold felt about ¼ inch in diameter for the bear's nose. Glue in place. Let dry.
4. Cut out a red felt mouth, glue in place, and let dry.
5. Glue 2 wiggle eyes or eyes cut out of felt in place. Let dry.
6. Cut out 2 circles of brown felt about ½ inch in diameter. Cut 2 smaller circles of light blue felt. Glue the light blue felt circles inside the brown circles of felt for ears. Glue ears on each side of bear's head. Hold in place for a minute and let dry.

Bear's Body

1. Make a body with the two 10-inch-square felt pieces as described on page 78. Glue felt body to bear's head.
2. Trace the paws, tummy, and bow tie from the design section of book onto tracing paper. Trace on felt and cut out. Glue in place and let dry.

BIRD

What You Need

Materials	Tools
Materials	*Tools*
1 plaster-filled eggshell head	pencil
2 pieces of blue felt, 10 by 10 inches	embroidery needle
2 wiggle eyes	scissors
dyed blue feathers—arts and crafts store	paintbrush
scrap of red felt	
thin piece of cardboard	
1 sheet tracing paper	
yellow acrylic paint	
glue	
embroidery thread	
carbon paper	
tracing paper	

Bird's Head

1. With pencil and tracing paper, trace and transfer beak pattern from the design section of book onto a thin piece of cardboard. Cut out beak. Bend cardboard along dotted lines. Apply glue to the back of the two bent sides of beak. Place beak on eggshell head and hold for a minute. Let dry.
2. Paint beak with yellow acrylic paint. Let dry.
3. Cut 10–15 blue feathers into 1-inch pieces.
4. Smear a layer of glue on the top half of eggshell head. Stick feathers in glue, working from top to bottom of head. Apply glue as necessary to completely cover head with feathers.

86

5. Glue 2 wiggle eyes or eyes cut of felt on each side of beak. Let dry.

Bird's Body

1. Make a body with the blue 10-inch-square felt pieces as described on page 78. Glue bird's head to felt body.
2. Cut a bow tie out of red felt, using pattern. Glue bow tie to bird's body just below the beak. Let dry.

KING

What You Need

Materials

1 plaster-filled eggshell head
2 pieces of red felt, 10 by 10 inches
scraps of felt in green, yellow, blue, gold,
   light blue, fuchsia, black
2 wiggle eyes
toilet paper tube
red acrylic paint
embroidery thread or yarn
black dyed straw

Tools

pencil
ruler
embroidery needle
paintbrush

King's Head

1. Cut 20 pieces of black dyed straw 4 inches
   long.
2. Using a scissor blade, curl both ends of each
   straw piece up as you would a piece of ribbon.

3. Apply a line of glue to the back of plaster-filled eggshell head, from top to bottom. Place each straw individually on gluey head. Press in place so that the straw hair hangs evenly on each side of face. Let dry.

4. To make a moustache, cut 6 pieces of straw 1 inch long. Tie them in a bundle, using another piece of straw, and secure the bundle with a knot. Cut off excess straw at knot.

5. Glue 2 wiggle eyes on face. Let dry. Glue moustache below eyes. Let dry.

King's Robe

1. Make a robe with the red 10-inch-square felt pieces as described on page 78. Glue king's head to felt body. Let dry.

2. Use several bright colors of felt for the details on robe. Do not worry if the details on each side are not exactly the same size, but the colors should be the same. Use the final sketch

of puppet king as an example for robe details,
or make up your own. Use plenty of glue to
secure the felt pieces to robe. Let dry.

QUEEN

What You Need

Materials
1 plaster-filled eggshell head
2 pieces of fuchsia felt, 10 by 10 inches
scraps of felt in yellow, green,
   turquoise, orange, and red
black dyed straw
toilet paper tube
2 wiggle eyes
red acrylic paint
glue
embroidery thread

Tools
pencil
ruler
paintbrush
knife
embroidery needle

Queen's Head

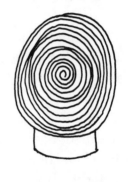

1. Smear a layer of glue on the top and back of a plaster-filled eggshell head. Place a strand of straw 3 feet long on top of the gluey head and coil it around, covering the back of the head. Press in place so that the eggshell is not showing through the hair. Let dry.

2. (optional) Cut a piece of dyed straw 6 inches long. Wrap the strand around a pencil in the same place about 12 times to make a bun of hair. Carefully slide it off the pencil, keeping it intact.

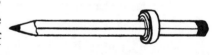

3. Tie the circle of straw with another piece of straw in a tight knot. Cut off straw at knot. Glue the bun at the top back of queen's head.

4. Glue 2 wiggle eyes in place. Let dry.

5. Cut a mouth out of red felt, or with a small

brush paint a mouth with red water color or acrylic paint.

Queen's Robe

1. Make a robe with the 10-inch-square fuchsia felt pieces as described on page 78. Glue head to robe.
2. Use the final sketch of the queen as an example for the details on the robe, or make up your own. Use bright colors of felt. Do not worry about making the symmetrical details exactly the same. Glue details on robe. Let dry.

Making a Crown (king or queen)

1. Mark 1 inch from the end of a toilet paper tube. Place tube on a cutting board. Hold the tube, and with a knife carefully cut through tube at mark. The 1-inch piece of tube will be the crown.
2. With scissors, make a cut in crown.
3. Then cut deep zigzags in it, leaving about ¼-inch band of cardboard at the bottom of crown.
4. Paint the crown inside and out with red acrylic paint. Let dry.
5. Place a line of glue on the bottom inside edge of crown. Fit the crown on puppet's head so the glue adheres crown to eggshell head. Let dry.

93

Tea Set

This miniature tea set will fit right in with your toys on a shelf, or it can be used for pretend tea parties. Left plain white, it looks like a simple oriental tea set. Painted, it can look like any type of china or pottery you like. It might be fun to go to a department store and get ideas for the painted designs from some of the traditional French and English china sets, or use the sample designs in the design section of the book.

What You Need

Materials

6 raw eggs
1 cup plaster of paris
½ cup plus 1 tablespoon water
1 sheet tracing paper
1 sheet medium sandpaper
4 white buttons with center ½ inch
   in diameter
empty egg carton
shellac
rubbing alcohol
acrylic paints
carbon paper
paper plate or scrap of cardboard
thin cardboard

Tools

pencil
ruler
scissors
wide elastic band
small paintbrush
flat nylon brush, 1 inch wide

Making a Teapot

1. Hollow out an egg.
2. Mark ½ inch from the narrow end of egg. Starting at the narrow end of egg, gradually and evenly break the shell down to mark.

3. Draw two marks along the top of eggshell ½ inch apart. Draw another mark ½ inch down from the center of the two marks. Draw straight lines connecting all 3 marks to form a triangle. Carefully break the eggshell out between the lines. This triangular notch will hold the tea spout.

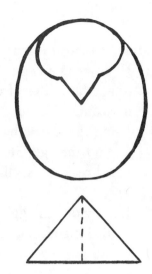

4. Cut a cardboard triangle, measuring 1 inch along the bottom and ¾ inch on either side. Fold the cardboard triangle in half. Unfold. Glue it in the notch of tea pot with the pointed end out. This is the spout.

5. For a lid, hollow out an egg.
6. Mark ¾ inch from the wide end of hollow egg. Start at the narrow end of egg and carefully break shell off evenly to the mark. The remaining piece should fit on the teapot.

7. Trace and transfer a design from the design section of book to the sides of the teapot.

95

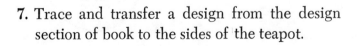

Making a Sugar Bowl

1. Hollow out an egg.
2. Mark the center of egg. Place an elastic band horizontally around center of egg at mark. Using the elastic band as a guide, draw a line around the egg. Starting at the narrow end of egg, break the shell off evenly down to center line.
3. Hollow out an egg.
4. Mark 1 inch from the wide end of egg. Starting at the narrow end, break the shell off evenly to mark. The remaining piece should fit on the sugar bowl.

Making Teacups

1. Hollow out 2 eggs.
2. Mark the center of each egg. Place an elastic band horizontally around the center at mark. Using it as a guide, draw a line around egg. Remove elastic. Repeat on second egg.
3. Starting at the wide end of each eggshell, carefully break off eggshell evenly to center line. Repeat on second egg.

Completing Tea Set

1. Mix 1 cup plaster of paris with ½ cup plus 1 tablespoon water in an empty can. Using the 1 inch wide nylon brush, paint the inside walls of all tea set pieces about 1/16 inch thick. Let dry overnight in an empty egg carton.

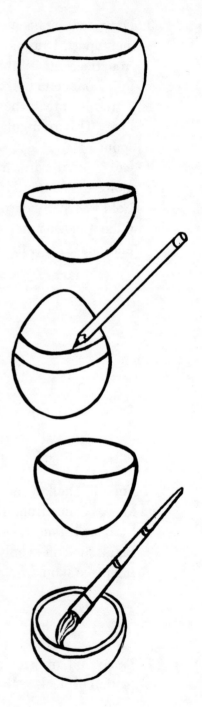

2. Place a piece of medium sandpaper on a hard, flat surface. Put each piece of the tea set broken side down on sandpaper and rub gently back and forth until the edges are flat and smooth.

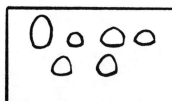

3. Glue a button to the bottom center of the teapot, sugar bowl, and 2 teacups. Let dry.

4. Trace and transfer a design from the design section of book onto each piece. The design from the book will need to be traced on both sides of the teacups, sugar bowl, and teapot. Be careful to line up the design, so that it is straight on each piece.

5. Paint the design with acrylic paint. Let dry. Paint the spout of the teapot with white acrylic paint. Let dry.

6. Paint all the pieces on the outside with shellac for a more finished appearance. Let dry. Rinse brush to clean it with rubbing alcohol.

Modern Furniture

Send your dolls or other toy figures on a flight to the moon in this ultramodern round furniture or just add the pieces to your display shelf. The roundness of an egg is the only defining detail of each piece. Once you find out how easy and fast it is to make eggshell furniture, you will come up with many designs of your own.

What You Need

Materials

4 raw eggs
2 cups plaster of paris
1¼ cups water
an empty soup or coffee can
1 sheet medium sandpaper
4 white buttons with ½-inch center
glue

Tools

flat nylon brush, 1 inch wide
wide elastic band
pencil

Table
1. Hollow out an egg.
2. Mark the center of the egg. Place an elastic band horizontally around egg at mark. Using the elastic band as a guide, draw a line around egg. Remove elastic.
3. Starting at the narrow end of egg, gradually break eggshell off to the center line.

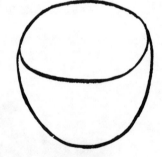

Couch
1. Hollow out an egg.
2. Place the elastic band vertically around egg. Using it as a guide, draw a line around egg from one hole to the other hole. Parallel to the

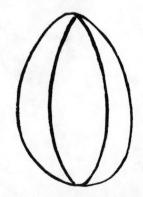

first line, draw another line 1½ inches away.

3. Carefully break the shell out between the two lines, so that ⅔ of the hollow egg is left. Your egg should have an oval shaped opening. Don't worry if the eggshell breaks off a little bit beyond the line; it can be sanded smooth and straight later.

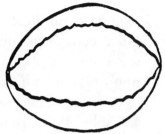

High-backed Chair

1. Hollow out an egg.
2. Mark ½ inch from the wide end of the hollow egg. Draw an oval on the egg with the top of the oval touching the hole at the narrow end and the bottom of the oval touching the ½-inch mark. With thumb and forefinger, carefully break out the shell inside of the oval. The narrow end will be the top of the chair and the wide end will be filled with plaster to make a seat.

Low-backed Chair

1. Hollow out an egg.
2. Mark the egg 1 inch down from the narrow end and ¾ inch below that.

3. Starting at the hole at the narrow end of eggshell, break it off evenly down to the 1-inch mark. Break a U-shaped opening in the remaining shell so that the bottom of the U touches the second mark.

Finishing the Furniture

1. Mix 2 cups of plaster of paris with 1¼ cups water in an empty can.
2. Apply plaster with a nylon brush to each of the furniture pieces in the following ways:

    a. Table—Fill the entire half-shell with plaster of paris, using the nylon brush or a spoon. Place in an empty egg carton and let dry for 2 days.

    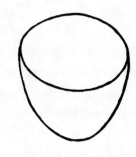

    b. Couch—Place the eggshell on its side. Paint the plaster on the top inside shell about ¹⁄₁₆ inch thick. Fill the bottom of the shell with plaster until it is level with the lower outside edge of the eggshell. This will be the seat. Place couch in empty egg carton and let dry for 2 days.

    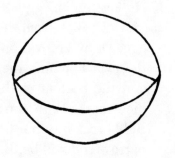

    c. High-backed Chair—Paint plaster of paris on inside of shell about ¹⁄₁₆ inch thick, using a flat nylon brush. Fill the bottom wide end of chair with plaster up to the edge of the oval, using the nylon brush or a spoon. Level plaster to make a flat seat. Place chair in empty egg carton and let dry for 2 days.

    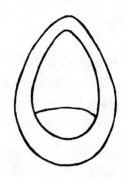

    d. Low-backed Chair—Paint plaster ¹⁄₁₆ inch thick in the inside of chair, using the nylon brush. Fill the bottom of the chair as above. Level plaster to make a flat seat. Place chair in empty egg carton and let dry for 2 days.

Finishing Furniture

1. Place a sheet of medium sandpaper on a hard, flat surface. Place the miniature table broken side down on the sandpaper and rub it gently back and forth until the table top is smooth and flat.
2. Sand the edges of the other pieces of furniture slowly with a small piece of sandpaper, taking care that the eggshell does not chip.
3. Glue a button on the bottom center of each piece of furniture. Let dry.

Stage Set

A stage set can be many different scenes, but this one could be used with the puppets in the book or with miniature figures of people or animals that you might have around the house. The eggshells are used to give the objects dimension. If you have a specific story in mind that you would like to make a stage set for, read through the directions that follow, then improvise your own ideas, using eggshells to create the objects that you need. Perhaps you would like to make an interior house scene, with a hanging lamp, furniture, swing, or something like caves, sand dunes, or woods with all eggshell trees. Look at an egg and see what ideas it suggests to you.

The aluminum foil on the interior sides of the stage reflects the landscape and makes it appear to continue beyond the box. You could also eliminate the foil and paint the sides of the stage as an alternative.

What You Need

Materials
2 dozen eggs
acrylic paints or poster paints
1 box, any size suitable (this one is 16 by
    24 inches and is 12 inches deep)
Scotch tape
brown paper tape
aluminum foil
glue

Tools
knife
paintbrush
scissors

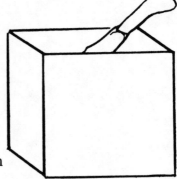

Making a Stage
1. Cut one wide side of a box completely off with a knife. Discard side.

2. Cut off half of the top side of box.

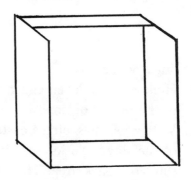

3. Secure the remaining top of box to the sides with brown paper tape.

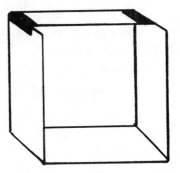

4. You will need 2 pieces of aluminum foil for the 2 interior sides of the stage. To measure the size of the foil needed, place it on the outside of the box. Cut the foil to the desired size and keep it as free of bends and wrinkles as possible.

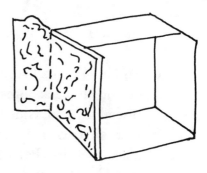

5. Tape the foil to the interior sides of stage with Scotch tape. Take 8 pieces of tape, bend them in half with the sticky side of tape out. Put a piece in each corner. Carefully place the foil on tape to completely cover both interior sides of stage. Smooth the foil in place.

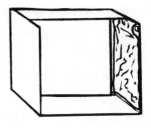

103

Making a Scene

1. Hollow out 2 dozen eggshells or collect them over a period of time.

2. With a pencil, sketch a castle on the back wall of the stage. Notice that it covers about one third the back area. The lines and details do not have to be perfectly straight. Use this one as an example, but feel free to make any changes in the design.

3. Paint as desired.

4. Paint the sky halfway down the back of the box and around the castle, using acrylic or poster paints and a paint brush. Let dry.

5. Paint part of the floor of the stage green to resemble grass, and another part blue to make a pond on one side. Let dry.

6. To glue eggshell scenery on it, lay the stage flat on its back. Break an eggshell down to resemble a sun. Glue it in the sky by applying glue on edge of eggshell and putting it in place. Let dry. Paint sun, using acrylic paint and a brush. Let dry.

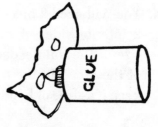

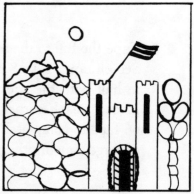

7. To make the mountains and hills, break 6–8 eggshells for the peaks. Glue them to the box round side down so that they resemble rocky

peaks. To make the hills, glue long half-shells down to box, round side up. Let dry completely.

8. Use 5 half-shells for branches and leaves to make the tree. Make the trunk out of 4 pieces of eggshells broken to resemble a trunk. Glue in place. Let dry.

9. Paint the mountain peaks by mixing ultramarine blue and brown paint together. As you paint them leave a little white showing through to look like snow on the peaks. The mountain gets gradually browner, then green toward the hills at the bottom. Paint the tree trunk brown. To paint the leaves, dab specks of yellow and green on and around the eggshells.

10. (optional) Paint the exterior of the stage set, using acrylic or poster paints and a brush. Let dry.

Sailboat

This sturdy little sailboat has a swinging boom to catch the wind just like a real sailboat. The boom is a rod which is horizontal and attached to the sail. It moves back and forth so that the sail can catch the wind and move forward. You can sail it on a shelf, but it will sink in a stream or bathtub because the body of the boat is made of plaster of paris. It is easy to make and requires very few materials.

What You Need

Materials

1 raw egg
½ cup plaster of paris
¼ cup plus 1 tablespoon water
an empty can
wire—white plastic-coated, or
   2 straight twigs, one 3 inches long,
   the other 4 inches long
small piece of felt
red acrylic paint
heavy thread or string
1 sheet tracing paper

Tools

spoon
wire cutters
pencil
ruler
paintbrush
scissors

Making a Boat

1. Hollow out an egg.
2. Draw a vertical line around the center of egg. Break one half of the eggshell off gradually to the line, leaving a long half-shell for the body of the boat.
3. Mix ½ cup plaster of paris with ¼ cup plus 1 tablespoon water in an empty can. Spoon the

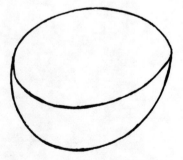

106

plaster into the half eggshell. Let it stand for about 15 minutes or until the plaster is solid but soft. Scoop the inside of boat out, leaving a platform in the center for the sail pole and bow at the end of the sailboat. Pierce the center of the platform with the pointed end of a pencil to make the hole that will hold the pole for the sail.

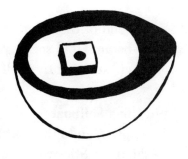

Making a Sail

1. With wire cutters, cut 2 pieces of wire, one 3 inches long, another 4 inches long. You can use thin twigs in place of wire. Mark ¾ inch from one end of each wire or twig.
2. With scissors, cut a piece of heavy thread or thin string 6 inches long.

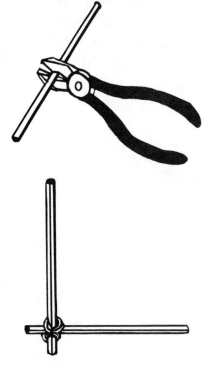

3. Place and hold the 2 wires together at marks in a right angle. Wrap the thread around the wires in a crisscross or X pattern over and over again to tie the wires tightly together. Apply glue to thread and hold the end in place until dry. The boom is the 3-inch wire that is horizontal to the sail pole.

4. Trace over the sail pattern in design section of book. Cut pattern out. Place pattern on a piece of felt. Trace around it; then cut out sail.
5. Attach the sail to wire pole that is 4 inches long and wire boom 3 inches long by wrapping the felt around the pole and gluing it in place. Let dry. Pierce the pointed end of felt sail with

the end of the boom and apply glue to the end of boom. Hold sail in place for a moment until it will stay put by itself. Let dry.

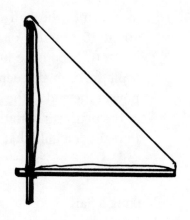

Finishing Sailboat

1. Apply glue to the bottom end of the pole with sail on it. Stick the pole in the hole of platform. Hold for a moment until the pole will stand up by itself. Let dry.
2. Paint the exterior of boat, the bow, and the center platform with red acrylic paint. Let dry.

Designs and Patterns

Parrot Eggshell Mosaic

Fish Eggshell Mosaic

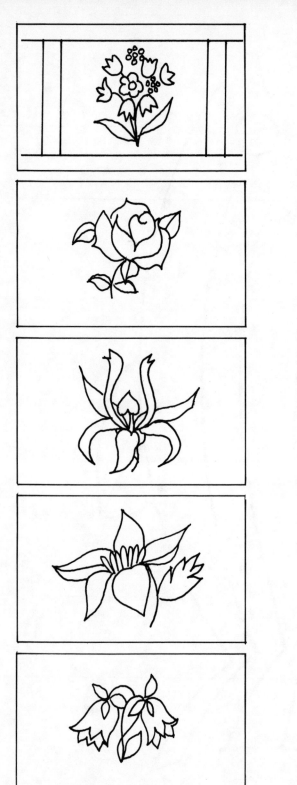

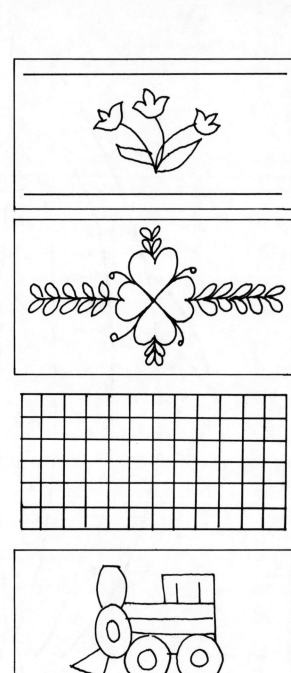

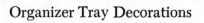

Organizer Tray Decorations

Herb Pot Decorations

Candlestick Holder Decorations

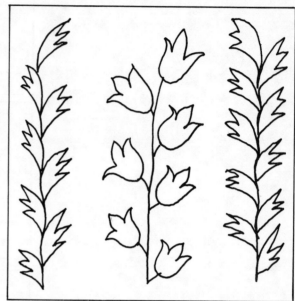

Necklace Decorations

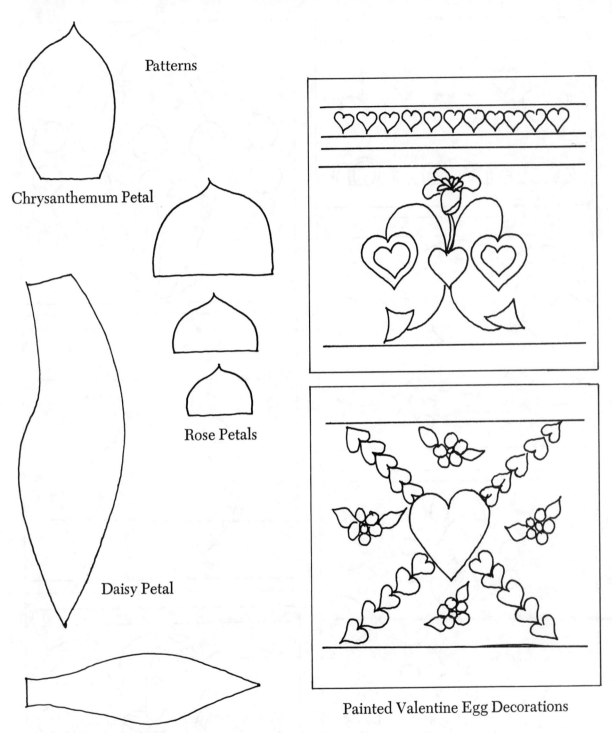

Patterns

Chrysanthemum Petal

Rose Petals

Daisy Petal

Daffodil Petal

Painted Valentine Egg Decorations

115

Painted Valentine Egg Decorations

Painted Birthday Egg Decorations

Painted Easter Egg Decorations

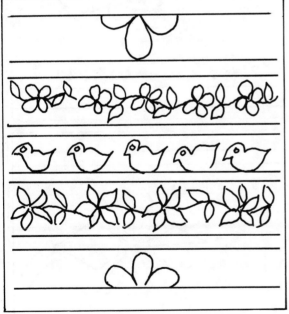

117

Painted Christmas Egg
and Tree Ornament Decorations

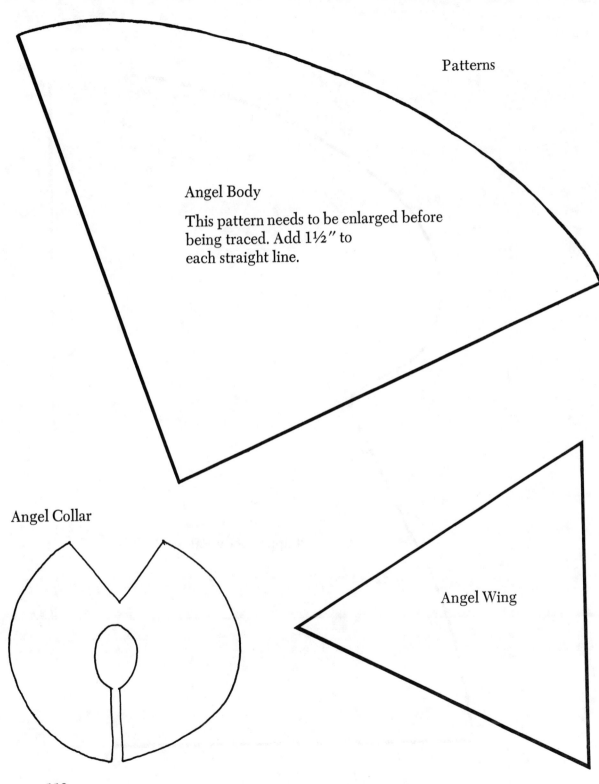

Patterns

Angel Body

This pattern needs to be enlarged before being traced. Add 1½″ to each straight line.

Angel Collar

Angel Wing

119

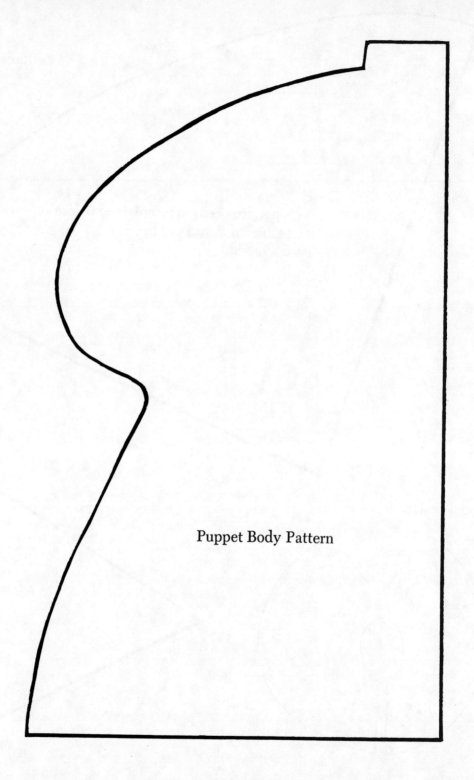

Puppet Body Pattern

Lion Puppet's Nose

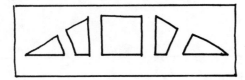

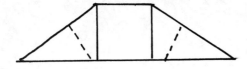

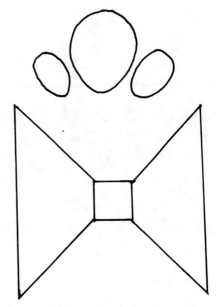

Lion Puppet's Bow Tie & Paws

Bear Puppet's Bow Tie & Paws

Bear Puppet's Tummy

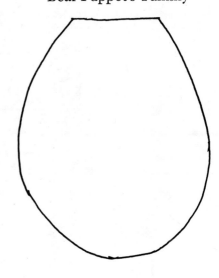

Bird Puppet's Beak

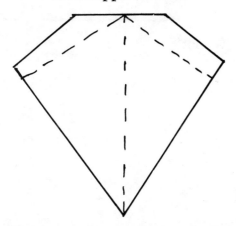

Patterns

Tea Set Decorations

Teapot

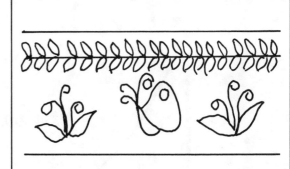

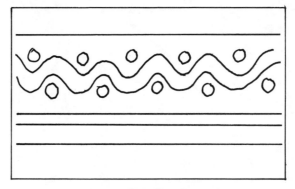

Sugar Bowl & Cups

Lid for Teapot & Sugar Bowl

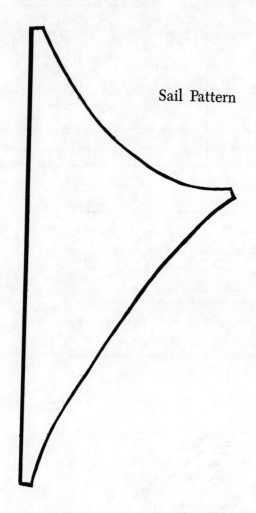

Sail Pattern

Index